contents

All About Curries   6

Ingredients   9

Equipment   11

Preparing chilies and curry pastes   12

Appetizers   16

Duck and Chicken   23

Fish and Seafood   31

Beef, Pork and Lamb   38

Fruit and Vegetables   44

Rice and Breads   48

Accompaniments   54

Glossary   58

Index   59

Guide to Weights and Measures   61

curries

THE ESSENTIAL KITCHEN

curries

The most common misconception about curry is that it is a single spice that is extremely hot. But a curry is so much more than a single element and curries are as varied in flavor as they are in color and spice combinations.

Curries needn't be excruciatingly hot any more than they need to come as a powder from a supermarket shelf or, indeed, to trace their ancestry exclusively to India. The word "curry" comes from the southern Indian, Tamil word "karhi", meaning "sauce" but, even then, it denotes a fairly liquid, not necessarily hot, sauce.

Thanks to the commercial and cultural links established thousands of years ago by Indian traders and religious practitioners, Indian culinary traditions were adopted, adapted, modified and assimilated into the cuisines of Southeast Asia well before the advent of the Christian era. So, the word "curry" could just as well apply to a spicy rendang from Indonesia or a succulent Thai fish cake as it could to a traditional, furnace-like Indian vindaloo.

Curries embrace a whole range of dishes, each distinctly different according to its spices and herbs and the combinations used. Curry connoisseurs can identify the country or region a dish comes from by the ingredients used.

Climate plays an important role in the food of a region, so where wheat grows, the curries tend to be dryer and the sauces thicker. Meals may be accompanied by chapatis, naan and unleavened breads. In rice-growing areas, curries tends to be more liquid, with rice the main ingredient of the meal, topped by a small amount of meat or vegetable sauce.

Originally, curry spices were used as preservatives and for their medicinal properties. Today, they are used mainly for flavoring and to make food more attractive, by providing color. Turmeric, which makes food yellow, is used to color rice and white vegetables such as cauliflower and potato. Coriander leaves and green chilies define Thailand's famous green curries, while red spices give dishes a vivid color and a sharp, pungent flavor.

When it comes to taste, spices provide an endless variety of possibilities, while rice and wheat-based breads rival each other as accompaniments. Indian cuisine uses ghee and yogurt extensively, with spicing being elaborate but not always hot. Wheat flour consumed in the form of chapatis accompanies the meal. Bangladeshi cuisine enjoys pungent spices, and seafood or other main ingredients cooked in oil, rather than ghee.

Southern Indian dishes use the region's plentiful coconuts, rice, chilies and mustard seeds to compose the meal. Thai cuisine favors a combination of cilantro (coriander), ginger, chilies and peppercorns. Its curries are generally coconut milk-based and accompanied by rice. In Indonesia, curries based on coconut milk are made fragrant with lemongrass and, often hot spices.

And we shouldn't forget that different regions have different food taboos. Hindus don't eat beef, Muslims avoid pork and Buddhists are vegetarians.

When it comes to grinding spices, we tend today to reach for the blender or an unemployed coffee grinder. However, spices were once ground on a flat, rectangular stone with a stone rolling pin. In India, it's still common to see spice-grinders standing on street corners pounding spices in giant mortars, throwing the heavy pestle with skill and ease, making passers by sneeze as the finely powdered spices fly into the hot air. For that ultimately authentic touch, a more manageable kitchen-size mortar and pestle set will produce just as genuine a result in your own home.

The combination of spice blends in Asia is endless, with each cook following their own taste and regional preference. There's only one proviso: the end product, be it curry or korma, must be a perfect blend. No one spice should be so strong as to dominate the dish, unless the cook deliberately wants it to. More than one hundred spices occur in Asian cooking. Fortunately, the most important of them are widely available in the West. Here are some of the essentials.

Turmeric is a hard, yellow root which is ground to a fine powder. Because of its appetizing flavor, it can be used alone or in combination with other spices and herbs. Cumin seeds form a sharp-tasting spice and can be purchased whole or ground. Coriander seeds are a delightful spice which adds flavor and aroma to a dish. They are available whole or ground. Cloves, nutmeg, mace, mustard seeds and pepper are also commonly used. Garam masala is a combination of spices often encountered in Indian dishes. No two recipes for it are the same, but it usually contains a blend of black pepper, cardamom, cinnamon, cloves and cumin seeds.

Garlic and onions are used fairly universally in curries to provide flavor and to give the sauce its body. Chilies are the vital ingredient in many curries. Fresh green or red, or in the form of dried red chilies, they can be mild or fiery, so should be used with discretion.

Fresh herbs such as cilantro (coriander), mint, curry leaves and basil are used in many Southeast Asian curries.

In addition to vinegar and lemon juice, the most commonly used souring agent is tamarind. A bean-like seed pod, tamarind is sold dried, as a pulp (puree) form, or as a concentrated liquid.

In this book we travel far and wide to sample the many curry styles of Asia. You'll taste many authentic and innovative recipes from Thailand, Sri Lanka, India, Burma, and Indonesia.

Another important aim of this book is to show just how easy it is to prepare and cook traditional Asian homemade curries. As a result, the recipes given will generally make quantities suitable for two people as a main meal with rice.

For special occasions, however, you could select a number of dishes for a genuine, multi-dish Asian-style curry meal. Remember, cooking curries ahead of time and leaving them to mature and develop their flavors can only improve the result. Provide plenty of rice and/or breads and arrange your curries and accompaniments around them. With the rice or bread as the base, encourage your guests to sample the curries one at a time, so they can appreciate the individual spicing of each dish served.

Before you sit down to your curry meal, though, forget Western proportions: lots of meat and a few vegetables are not the route to success with curries. Rice and/or bread form the main part of the meal, with meat, fish, chicken or vegetable curries being served in small quantities. When eating Indian breads, you should go traditional and eat with your fingers. Tear off a portion of bread and use it to scoop up some curry or accompaniment. In certain parts of Asia, the right hand only is used for eating, use of the left being considered impolite, but the experts all agree on one thing: curry does taste better when eaten with the fingers.

Cold water is the most authentic beverage to drink with a curry meal, because fizzy or carbonated drinks, including beer, tend to exaggerate the burning sensation of a hot curry. Surprisingly, so does iced water. Instead, opt for a lassi (yogurt and fruit-based drink, see page 57).

Curries represent the ingenious ways people from regions throughout Asia have found to incorporate local and imported ingredients to make some of the world's tastiest and best-loved meals.

Black cumin seeds: Available at Indian and Asian markets. Substitute black sesame seeds.

Cardamom: A member of the ginger family. The pods contain seeds with a strong lemony flavor. Also available ground.

Cinnamon sticks: Rolled pieces of the inner bark of the branches of a small evergreen tree. Native to Sri Lanka and India. They have a distinctive sweet flavor and aroma. Also available ground.

Cloves, whole: Dried unopened flower buds of a tropical evergreen tree. They have an extremely pungent sweet taste and aroma. Also available ground.

Coriander seeds: Tiny yellow-tan seeds from the cilantro (fresh coriander) plant. Used, whole or ground, as a spice. Flavor is reminiscent of lemon, sage, and caraway.

Cumin seeds: Dried, small, crescent-shaped seeds from a plant related to parsley. Available whole or ground, and in three colors: amber, white, and black. They have a powerful earthy, nutty flavor and aroma.

Green peppercorns: Unripened peppercorns with a soft texture and a fresh, sour flavor. Available freeze dried or pickled in brine or vinegar. Refrigerate after opening.

Mustard seeds: Seeds from a plant belonging to the cabbage family. Available in yellow, brown, or black.

Bay leaves: Dried leaves from a large, evergreen tree belonging to the laurel family, and native to the Mediterranean region. The leaves impart a lemon-nutmeg flavor. They are used in cooking, but are not edible.

Cilantro, fresh (fresh coriander): Green, lacy leaves from the coriander plant. They have a sharp, tangy, fresh flavor and aroma. Used in Asian, Mexican, and South American cuisines. Also known as Chinese parsley.

Curry leaves, fresh: Bright, shiny herb leaves used in Indian and Southeast Asian cuisines. Added to sauces, curries, and stir-fries, they impart a subtle curry flavor to the food.

Galangal, fresh: The rhizome of a plant native to Southeast Asia. It has reddish skin, orange or white flesh, and a peppery gingerlike flavor.

Ginger, fresh: The rhizome of a tall flowering tropical plant, native to China. It has tan skin, ivory to greenish yellow flesh, and a peppery, slightly sweet flavor, with notes of rosemary and lemon. Used fresh in sweet and savory cooking and beverages.

Kaffir lime leaves, fresh: The shiny dark green leaves of this citrus plant have an unusual figure-eight shape, formed by two leaves joined together. Sharply aromatic, they impart a citrus flavor. Traditionally used in Thai and Indonesian cuisines.

Lemongrass, fresh: A tropical grass with long greenish stalks. It has a strong lemonlike flavor and aroma. Peel off the outer layer of the fresh stalk, and use the white part, or the bulb, only. Bruise, chop, or slice the lemongrass as large pieces are not edible.

Mint, fresh: Herb with a fresh flavor and aroma, used in sweet and savory dishes and beverages.

Coffee/spice grinder: The smaller coffee/spice grinder is a quick and easy alternative to the mortar and pestle, as it grinds small quantities of dry hard spices. It is recommended you have a separate grinder for spices and a separate grinder for coffee as the strong spice flavors will remain in the basin of the grinder.

Electric food processor: A food processor is used for blending already ground spices and fresh herbs together.

Mortar and pestle: Usually made from stone, wood or ceramic, the mortar and pestle is a manual tool for grinding herbs and spices. This indispensable duo comes in varying sizes. The pestle is pounded and rotated against the sides of the bowl-shaped mortar, to crush and grind fresh, dried and roasted herbs and spices. Once you get used to using a mortar and pestle, it is often quicker than using a food processor. It also saves on washing up time.

Wok: The wok is a great addition to the kitchen. Its size and classic shape are especially suitable for cooking curries and deep-frying pappadams and savories. You will need a lid for the wok or you can cover the wok with aluminum foil. A medium-sized lidded saucepan will make a good substitute for cooking curries.

Coffee/spice grinder

Electric food processor

Mortar and pestle

Wok

curry pastes

Preparation of a fresh chili

Take special care not to touch your face or eyes when handling chilies, and always wash your hands thoroughly with soap and hot water afterwards. Alternatively, wear disposable gloves.

1 Using a sharp knife, trim the stem from the chili.

2 Cut the chili in half lengthwise.

3 Scrape the seeds and the white pith (membrane) from the skin. The seeds contain some heat, but the real source of heat is the capsaicin, found in the white pith. Some recipes leave in the seeds for a hotter flavor.

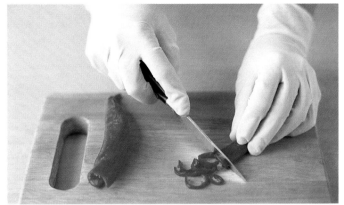

4 Slice or chop the chili as required.

Bird's eye chilies, red or green: Also known as Thai (bird) chilies. Blazing hot, with a clear fiery taste. Use fresh in small quantities. Substitute small amounts of jalapeño or serrano chilies.

Chili pepper flakes: Available in bottles, or coarsely crush small, dried red peppers.

Chili powder: Available in bottles, or grind small, dried red chili peppers or red chili pepper flakes.

Preparation of a curry paste

1 In a small skillet, combine chilies, peppercorns, cumin seeds, paprika, and shrimp paste and stir over medium heat until fragrant, 30–60 seconds.

2 Remove from heat and let cool. Transfer to a food processor.

3 Add remaining ingredients and process to a smooth paste.

4 Spoon into a sterilized jar and seal. Store in refrigerator for up to 3 weeks.

Dried red chilies: Includes large or small chilies. Sold in Asian stores in bags or packets.

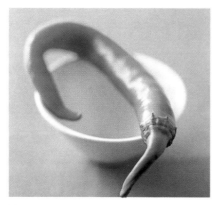

Thai chili, green: Also known as Thai dragon chili. Medium-hot chili, grows up to 1½ inches (4 cm) long. Commonly used fresh in Asian cooking. Slightly milder green Anaheim chili pepper may be substituted.

Thai chili, red: The ripe counterpart to the Thai green chili is also medium-hot and up to 1½ inches (4 cm) long. Red Anaheim chili pepper may be substituted.

Thai red curry paste

6 red bird's eye or Thai (bird) chilies, seeded and coarsely chopped

2 teaspoons black peppercorns

2 teaspoons cumin seeds

1 teaspoon sweet paprika

1 teaspoon dried shrimp paste

1 red onion, coarsely chopped

2 stalks lemongrass (white part only), chopped

4 cloves garlic, chopped

1 tablespoon grated fresh galangal

2 tablespoons coarsely chopped fresh cilantro (fresh coriander)

2 tablespoons vegetable oil

2 teaspoons fish sauce

In a small skillet, combine chilies, peppercorns, cumin seeds, paprika, and shrimp paste and stir over medium heat until fragrant, 30–60 seconds. Remove from heat and let cool. Transfer to a food processor. Add remaining ingredients and process to a smooth paste. Spoon into a sterilized jar and seal. Store in refrigerator for up to 3 weeks.

Makes about 1 cup (8 fl oz / 250 ml)

Thai green curry paste

1 tablespoon coriander seeds

1 tablespoon cumin seeds

4 black peppercorns

1 cup (1⅓ oz / 40 g) coarsely chopped fresh cilantro (fresh coriander)

2 fresh kaffir lime leaves, shredded

6 cloves garlic, chopped

4 scallions (shallots / spring onions), including green parts, coarsely chopped

4 fresh green Thai or Anaheim chilies, seeded and coarsely chopped

1 tablespoon grated fresh galangal

1 teaspoon dried shrimp paste

2 stalks lemongrass (white part only), chopped

2 teaspoons fish sauce

2 tablespoons vegetable oil

In a small skillet, combine coriander, cumin seeds, and peppercorns and stir over medium heat until fragrant, about 1 minute. Empty into a bowl and let cool. Transfer to a spice or coffee grinder and grind to a fine powder. Transfer to a food processor and add remaining ingredients. Process to a smooth paste. Spoon into a sterilized jar and seal. Store in the refrigerator for up to 3 weeks.

Makes about 1½ cups (12 fl oz / 375 ml)

Garam masala

1 tablespoon cardamom seeds (not pods)

2 cinnamon sticks, broken up

1 teaspoon black peppercorns

1 teaspoon cloves

1 teaspoon cumin seeds

1 teaspoon fennel seeds

I n a small skillet, combine all ingredients and stir over medium heat for about 1 minute, or until fragrant. Empty into a bowl and let cool. Transfer to a spice or coffee grinder and grind to a fine powder. Store in a tightly sealed jar in a cool, dark place for up to 4 weeks.

Makes about ¼ cup (2 fl oz / 60 ml)

Penang curry paste

8 dried red chilies

¼ cup (2 fl oz / 60 ml) boiling water

4 scallions (shallots/spring onions)

6 cloves garlic, chopped

2 stalks lemongrass (white part only), chopped

3 cilantro (fresh coriander) roots, coarsely chopped

1 tablespoon peeled and grated fresh ginger

1 teaspoon ground coriander

1 teaspoon ground cumin

2 tablespoons roasted peanuts

2 tablespoons vegetable oil

P ut chilies in a small bowl and add boiling water to cover. Let soak for 5 minutes. Drain. Chop chilies coarsely. Transfer to a food processor and add all remaining ingredients. Process to a thick paste. Spoon into a sterilized jar and seal. Store in the refrigerator for up to 3 weeks.

Makes about ½ cup (4 fl oz / 125 ml)

Spicy dal

1 cup (7 oz / 220 g) red lentils

2 teaspoons peeled and grated fresh ginger

3 cloves garlic, finely chopped

1 fresh red bird's eye or Thai (bird) chili, seeded and chopped

1 stalk celery, chopped

2 tablespoons chopped fresh cilantro (fresh coriander)

1 tablespoon fresh lemon juice

5 cups (40 fl oz / 1.25 L) water

2 teaspoons tamarind paste

4 scallions (shallots/spring onions), chopped

1 medium carrot, chopped

1/2 teaspoon garam masala (see page 15)

1/4 teaspoon ground turmeric

1/4 teaspoon ground coriander

1 teaspoon cumin seeds

Rinse and pick over lentils. In a medium saucepan, combine lentils, ginger, garlic, chili, celery, cilantro, lemon juice, water, tamarind paste, scallions, and carrot. Stir, cover and bring to a boil over high heat. Reduce heat to low and simmer for 30–40 minutes, or until lentils are tender.

In a blender or food processor, puree the lentil mixture in batches until smooth. Return to saucepan.

In a small skillet, combine the remaining ingredients and stir over medium heat for about 1–2 minutes, or until fragrant. Add spice mixture to lentil mixture and stir to blend. Cook over low heat, stirring constantly, for 5 minutes, or until thickened. Serve warm or at room temperature, with curries and / or fried pappadams.

Serves 4

Hints

The term dal *generally refers to dried legumes, but the word dal indicates that the legume has been split. It also commonly refers to an Indian prepared dish of lentil puree. Spicy dal is served as part of an Indian meal or as an appetizer with pappadams or naan bread.*

Curried mixed nuts

In a wok or skillet, heat oil over medium heat. Add cashews and cook, stirring constantly, until lightly browned, 1–2 minutes. Using a slotted spoon, transfer to paper towels to drain. Repeat to fry almonds, then peanuts. Combine nuts in a medium bowl. Add remaining ingredients and stir until well combined. Serve at room temperature.

Makes 3 cups (15 oz/470 g)

3 tablespoons vegetable oil

1 cup (5 oz/150 g) cashew nuts

1 cup (5 oz/150 g) blanched whole almonds

1 cup (5 oz/150 g) raw peanuts

1 tablespoon sea salt

1 teaspoon garam masala (see page 15)

¹/₂ teaspoon chili powder

Hint

These tasty little morsels make a great snack to serve with drinks.

Shrimp fries

8 oz (250 g) jumbo shrimp (king prawns), shelled, deveined, and finely chopped

½ onion, finely chopped

3 cloves garlic, finely chopped

2 teaspoons peeled and grated fresh ginger

2 tablespoons chopped fresh cilantro (fresh coriander)

1 fresh red Thai or Anaheim chili, seeded and finely chopped

½ teaspoon ground cumin

½ teaspoon garam masala (see page 15)

2 tablespoons besan flour

2 tablespoons all-purpose (plain) flour

2 cups (16 fl oz/500 ml) vegetable oil for deep-frying

1 lime, cut into 8 wedges for serving

In a medium bowl, combine shrimp, onion, garlic, ginger, cilantro, chili, cumin, and garam masala. Stir until well combined. Divide into 8 portions and shape into balls. Roll in combined flours.

In a Dutch oven, wok, or deep fryer, heat oil to 375°F (190°C), or until a small bread cube dropped in the oil sizzles and turns golden in 1 minute. Add shrimp balls in batches and cook for 2–3 minutes, or until golden. Using a slotted spoon, transfer to paper towels to drain. Serve immediately, with lime wedges.

Makes 8

Hint

Shrimp fries are a great hors d'oeuvre, snack, or accompaniment to curry.

Thai curry fish cakes

In a food processor, combine fish, curry paste, fish sauce, garlic, egg, and brown sugar. Process to a thick paste. Transfer to a medium bowl. Add scallions, lemongrass, cilantro, lime leaves, and green beans. Mix until well combined. Shape into 16 patties. Place on a plate, cover, and refrigerate for 30 minutes.

In a large, heavy skillet, heat oil until surface shimmers and fry fish cakes in batches until golden, about 1 minute on each side. Using a slotted spoon, transfer to paper towels to drain. Serve immediately, with Thai sweet chili sauce.

Makes 16

1 lb (500 g) redfish or white sea bass fillets, coarsely chopped

1 tablespoon Thai red curry paste (see page 14 for recipe)

2 teaspoons fish sauce

2 cloves garlic, coarsely chopped

1 egg yolk

2 teaspoons packed brown sugar

2 scallions (shallots / spring onions), sliced

1 stalk lemongrass (white part only), finely sliced

2 tablespoons chopped fresh cilantro (fresh coriander)

4 fresh kaffir lime leaves, finely shredded

2 oz (60 g) green beans, trimmed and very thinly sliced

1 cup (8 fl oz / 250 ml) vegetable oil

1/2 cup (4 fl oz / 125 ml) Thai sweet chili sauce

Hint

As an alternative, make 32 smaller balls and serve with toothpicks as hors d'oeuvres.

Curry yogurt soup

2 tablespoons vegetable oil

1 green Thai or Anaheim chili,
 seeded and chopped

4 cloves garlic, finely chopped

1 tablespoon peeled and grated fresh ginger

4 dried red chilies

1 teaspoon cumin seeds

1/2 teaspoon chili powder

1/2 teaspoon ground turmeric

8 fresh curry leaves

2 cups (16 oz / 500 g) plain (natural) yogurt

sea salt to taste

1/2 cup (4 fl oz / 125 ml) coconut milk

1/4 fresh red Thai or Anaheim chili, seeded and
 cut into very fine 2-inch (5-cm) lengths

In a medium saucepan, heat 1 tablespoon of oil over medium heat and fry chili, garlic, ginger, dried chilies, cumin seeds, chili powder, turmeric, and 4 of the curry leaves for 2–3 minutes, or until fragrant. Reduce heat to low and stir in yogurt and salt. Cook for 5 minutes, stirring (do not boil). Stir in coconut milk and cook for 1 minute, stirring constantly. Remove and discard dried chilies. Spoon into serving bowls.

In a small skillet, heat remaining 1 tablespoon of oil and fry remaining 4 curry leaves and shredded fresh red chili until the chili curls, about 30 seconds. Using a slotted spoon, transfer to paper towels to drain. Garnish each soup bowl with curry and chili leaf mixture.

Serves 2

Curry vegetable spring rolls

In a wok or large skillet, heat oils over medium heat. Add cumin seeds, garlic, ginger, green chilies, turmeric and ground red pepper. Fry for 1 minute. Stir in potatoes, peas, and salt and fry for 1 minute. Remove from heat and let cool completely. Stir in cilantro and mint.

Place 1 wrapper on a work surface. Place 1 heaped tablespoon of filling in the center of wrapper. Fold over sides, and then roll up diagonally. Seal loose edge with egg white. Repeat with remaining wrappers and filling.

In a wok or deep fryer, heat oil to 375°F (190°C), or until a small bread cube dropped in the oil sizzles and turns golden in 1 minute. Add spring rolls in batches and fry until golden, about 2 minutes. Using a slotted spoon, transfer to paper towels to drain. Serve immediately with Thai sweet chili sauce and/or soy sauce.

Makes 12

1 tablespoon vegetable oil

2 teaspoons Asian sesame oil

1 teaspoon cumin seeds

1 clove garlic, finely chopped

1 tablespoon peeled and grated fresh ginger

2 green Thai or Anaheim chilies, seeded and finely chopped

1 teaspoon ground turmeric

1 teaspoon chili powder

1 lb (500 g) potatoes, peeled, boiled, and cut into $1/4$-inch (6-mm) dices

$1/2$ cup ($2^{1}/_{2}$ oz / 75 g) fresh or frozen peas

$1/2$ teaspoon sea salt

1 tablespoon chopped fresh cilantro (fresh coriander)

1 tablespoon chopped fresh mint

12 frozen spring roll wrappers, about 8 inches (20 cm), thawed

1 egg white, lightly beaten

3 cups (24 fl oz / 750 ml) vegetable oil for deep-frying

Thai sweet chili sauce and/or soy sauce for dipping

Rice flour crisps

1½ cups (12 oz / 375 g) rice flour

⅓ cup (2 oz / 60 g) besan flour

1 tablespoon cumin seeds

1 teaspoon chili powder

1 teaspoon ground coriander

2 tablespoons ghee

about 1 cup (8 fl oz / 250 ml) coconut milk

3 cups (24 fl oz / 750 ml) vegetable oil
  for deep-frying

2 teaspoons sea salt

Sift flours into a bowl. Add cumin seeds, chili powder and coriander. Rub ghee into dry ingredients, using your fingers. Make a well in the center and stir in enough coconut milk to make a soft batter. Spoon batter into a piping bag fitted with a ½-inch (12-mm) star tip.

In a large wok, heat oil to 375°F (190°C), or until a small bread cube dropped in the oil sizzles and turns golden in 1 minute. Working in batches, carefully pipe 2-inch (5-cm) lengths of batter into hot oil and fry until golden and crisp, about 1 minute. Using a slotted spoon, transfer to paper towels to drain. Sprinkle with salt and serve immediately. Serve as a snack or with drinks.

Serves 4

chicken

Chili-chicken curry

In a wok or skillet, heat oil over medium heat and fry bay leaves, cardamom, coriander, pepper flakes, onion, ginger, garlic, and chilies for 2–3 minutes, or until onion is soft. Stir in tomatoes and cook for 3 minutes, or until tomatoes are split. Add chicken and fry for 4–6 minutes, or until chicken becomes opaque. Add coconut milk and peppercorns. Reduce heat and simmer for 5–6 minutes, or until chicken is tender. Remove from heat and stir in cilantro. Serve with steamed basmati rice.

Serves 4

2 tablespoons vegetable oil

3 bay leaves

4 whole cardamom pods, bruised

1 tablespoon coriander seeds, crushed

2 teaspoons chili pepper flakes

1 onion, chopped

1 tablespoon peeled and grated fresh ginger

4 cloves garlic, finely chopped

1 large fresh red Thai or Anaheim chili, seeded and chopped

1 large fresh green Thai or Anaheim chili, seeded and chopped

4 tomatoes, peeled and chopped

1 lb (500 g) boneless, skinless chicken breast halves, cut into bite-sized pieces

1¹/₂ cups (12 fl oz / 375 ml) coconut milk

1 tablespoon green peppercorns

2 tablespoons chopped fresh cilantro (fresh coriander)

Duck and green chili curry

FOR SPICE PASTE

2 fresh green Thai or Anaheim chilies,
   coarsely chopped

1 onion, coarsely chopped

2 teaspoons ground turmeric

1 tablespoon ground coriander

1 tablespoon raw cashew nuts

2 teaspoons peeled and grated fresh ginger

4 cloves garlic, coarsely chopped

2 black peppercorns

2 tablespoons water

3 tablespoons vegetable oil

2 bay leaves

1 stalk lemongrass (white part only), bruised

1/2 teaspoon dried shrimp paste

1 lb (500 g) boneless duck or chicken breasts,
   with skin, cut into 1-inch (2.5-cm) cubes

1 cup (8 fl oz / 250 ml) water

1 tablespoon tamarind paste

16 basil leaves

To make spice paste: In a food processor, combine all ingredients and process to a thick paste. Scrape into a small bowl.

In a wok or large skillet, heat 2 tablespoons of oil over medium heat and fry spice paste for 1 minute, or until fragrant. Add bay leaves, lemongrass and shrimp paste. Stir-fry for 1 minute, add duck or chicken, and stir-fry for 4–5 minutes, or until opaque. Stir in 1 cup (8 fl oz / 250 ml) water, reduce heat to a simmer, and cook for 15 minutes, or until duck is tender. Remove from heat and stir in tamarind paste. Remove lemongrass.

In a small skillet, heat remaining 1 tablespoon of oil over medium heat and fry basil leaves in batches. Using a slotted spoon, transfer to paper towels to drain. Spoon curry into serving bowls and garnish each serving with fried basil leaves. Serve with steamed basmati rice.

Serves 4

Chicken vindaloo

To make marinade: In a baking dish, combine all the ingredients and stir to blend. Add chicken and toss to coat. Cover and refrigerate for 30 minutes.

In a wok or large skillet, heat oil over medium heat and fry onion and curry leaves until onions are soft, about 1 minute. Reduce heat, add chicken and marinade, and fry for 2 minutes. Add potato, cover, and simmer for 10 minutes or until potato and chicken are tender. Remove from heat and stir in green chilies.

Serves 4

FOR MARINADE

$^2/_3$ cup (5 fl oz / 160 ml) malt vinegar

1$^1/_2$ teaspoons coriander seeds, crushed

1 teaspoon cumin seeds, crushed

1 teaspoon chili powder

$^1/_4$ teaspoon ground turmeric

3 cloves garlic, finely chopped

1 teaspoon peeled and grated fresh ginger

1 teaspoon sea salt

1$^1/_2$ teaspoons sweet paprika

1 tablespoon tomato paste (puree)

pinch ground fenugreek

1$^1/_4$ cups (10 fl oz / 300 ml) water

1 lb (500 g) skinless, boneless chicken breast halves, cut into 1-inch (2.5-cm) cubes

1 tablespoon vegetable oil

1 onion, sliced

6 fresh curry leaves

1 large potato, peeled and cut into 1-inch (2.5-cm) cubes

2 green Thai or Anaheim chilies, seeded and finely chopped

Hint

This is a traditional hot Indian curry. Serve with steamed basmati rice or naan.

Tandoori chicken

4 chicken legs

4 chicken thighs

³/₄ cup (6 oz / 180 g) plain (natural) yogurt

1 teaspoon garam masala
   (see page 15 for recipe)

2 teaspoons peeled and grated fresh ginger

6 cloves garlic, finely chopped

¹/₄ teaspoon ground turmeric

1 teaspoon ground coriander

1 tablespoon fresh lemon juice

¹/₄ teaspoon Chinese powdered red food
   coloring (see glossary)

pinch sea salt

1 tablespoon vegetable oil

2 limes, quartered

Using a sharp knife, make 2 slits in skin side of each chicken piece. Place chicken pieces in a baking dish. In a small bowl, combine yogurt, garam masala, ginger, garlic, turmeric, coriander, lemon juice, red coloring, salt, and oil. Mix well. Pour over chicken pieces and toss to coat chicken. Cover and refrigerate for 2 hours.

Remove chicken from refrigerator 30 minutes before roasting. Preheat oven to 425°F (220°C). Transfer chicken to a roasting pan. Roast for 25 minutes, or until juices run clear when the chicken is pierced with a sharp knife. Remove from oven. Serve immediately, with lime wedges.

Serves 4

Hint

Tandoori chicken is traditionally cooked on a spit in a clay tandoor oven, but you can also prepare it in a regular oven.

Penang duck curry

In a large saucepan or wok, heat coconut cream over medium heat until oil separates from cream. Stir in curry paste, and cook until fragrant, about 1 minute. Add lime leaves and peas and cook for 1 minute. Stir in fish sauce, brown sugar, coconut milk, and duck. Stir over medium heat until duck is heated through, 3–4 minutes. Spoon into serving bowls and top with basil leaves. Serve with steamed jasmine rice.

Serves 2

$^1/_4$ cup (2 fl oz / 60 ml) coconut cream

$1^1/_2$ tablespoons Thai red curry paste
  (see page 14 for recipe)

3 fresh kaffir lime leaves

$^1/_2$ cup ($2^1/_2$ oz / 75 g) fresh or frozen green peas

2 teaspoons fish sauce

2 teaspoons packed brown sugar

$1^1/_2$ cups (12 fl oz / 375 ml) coconut milk

$^1/_2$ Chinese roast duck, cut into serving pieces

$^1/_4$ cup fresh basil leaves

Thai chicken and pumpkin curry

FOR SPICE PASTE

1/2 teaspoon chili pepper flakes

1 teaspoon ground coriander

1/4 teaspoon ground cumin

1/4 teaspoon ground turmeric

1/2 teaspoon ground cinnamon

1/4 teaspoon ground cloves

1/4 teaspoon ground star anise

2 cardamom pods, bruised

1 scallion (shallot / spring onion), chopped

1 teaspoon finely chopped fresh cilantro
   (fresh coriander) roots

2 cloves garlic, finely chopped

1-inch (2.5-cm) piece fresh galangal,
   peeled and finely chopped

2 fresh kaffir lime leaves, shredded

sea salt to taste

2 tablespoons vegetable oil

2 cloves garlic, finely chopped

1 1/2 cups (12 fl oz / 375 ml) coconut milk

1/2 cup (4 fl oz / 125 ml) chicken stock

1 lb (500 g) skinless, boneless chicken thighs,
   cut into strips 3/8-inch (1-cm) wide

2 teaspoons fish sauce

1 1/2 cups (8 oz / 250 g) cubed, peeled pumpkin

1 onion, sliced lengthwise

1/2 cup (3 oz / 90 g) unsalted
   roasted peanuts

1 tablespoon packed brown sugar

3 fresh kaffir lime leaves, shredded

3 tablespoons tamarind paste

1/2 fresh red Thai or Anaheim chili,
   seeded and cut into 1 1/2-inch (4-cm) shreds

To make spice paste: In a small skillet, combine pepper flakes, coriander, cumin, turmeric, cinnamon, cloves, star anise, and cardamom pods. Stir over medium heat for 1 minute, or until fragrant. Transfer to a food processor and add remaining ingredients. Process to a smooth paste.

In a wok or large skillet, heat oil over medium heat. Add garlic and spice paste and fry for 1–2 minutes, or until fragrant. Stir in coconut milk and broth, reduce heat, and simmer for 3 minutes. Add fish sauce and pumpkin. Cover and simmer for 5 minutes. Add chicken and simmer for 5–6 minutes, or until chicken and pumpkin are tender. Add onion, peanuts, brown sugar, lime leaves and tamarind paste. Simmer for 1 minute. Spoon into serving bowls and garnish with shredded chili. Serve with steamed jasmine rice.

Serves 4

Chicken and nut curry

To make spice paste: In a food processor, combine all ingredients and process for 30 seconds, or until smooth. Transfer to a small bowl.

In a wok or large skillet, heat oil over medium heat and fry spice paste until fragrant, about 2 minutes. Add apricots and chicken. Cook for 1 minute. Stir in broth, cover, and simmer over low heat for 10–12 minutes, or until chicken is tender. Spoon into serving bowls. Garnish with cashews and cilantro leaves. Serve with steamed basmati rice.

Serves 4

FOR SPICE PASTE

1 onion, coarsely chopped

1/3 cup (3 fl oz / 80 ml) tomato paste (puree)

1/3 cup (2 oz / 60 g) roasted cashew nuts

2 teaspoons garam masala
  (see page 15 for recipe)

3 cloves garlic, chopped

1 tablespoon fresh lemon juice

1 teaspoon grated lemon zest

1/4 teaspoon ground turmeric

1 teaspoon sea salt

1 tablespoon plain (natural) yogurt

2 tablespoons vegetable oil

3 oz (90 g) dried apricots

1 lb (500 g) skinless, boneless chicken thighs,
  cut into strips 3/8-inch (1-cm) wide

1 1/4 cups (10 fl oz / 300 ml) chicken broth

1/4 cup (1 1/2 oz / 45 g) roasted cashew nuts
  for garnish

1/4 cup (1/4 oz / 7 g) fresh cilantro
  (fresh coriander) leaves for garnish

Festive duck curry

1 tablespoon peeled and grated fresh ginger

4 cloves garlic, finely chopped

2 tablespoons rice vinegar

1 lb (500 g) boneless duck breast fillets, with skin, cut into strips 1/4-inch (6-mm) wide

2 tablespoons vegetable oil

1 onion, chopped

2 teaspoons ground cumin

2 teaspoons ground coriander

1 teaspoon chili powder

2 tomatoes, peeled and chopped

1 cup (8 fl oz / 250 ml) chicken broth

1 tablespoon fish sauce

1 teaspoon ground pepper

2 tablespoons chopped fresh cilantro (fresh coriander)

In a small bowl, combine ginger, garlic, and vinegar. Put duck in a baking dish. Add ginger mixture, and toss until well coated. Cover and refrigerate for 1 hour.

In a wok or large skillet, heat oil over medium heat and fry onion for 1 minute, or until soft. Add cumin, coriander, and chili powder. Fry for 1 minute. Add duck and marinade. Fry for 4–5 minutes, or until duck is opaque. Add tomatoes and stir-fry for 3 minutes. Stir in broth, fish sauce, and pepper. Reduce heat to low, cover, and simmer until duck is tender, 10–12 minutes. Stir in cilantro. Spoon into serving bowls. Serve with steamed jasmine rice

Serves 4

seafood

Thai red curry shrimp

Shell and devein shrimp, leaving tails intact and reserving shrimp heads. Wash shrimp heads. In a wok or large skillet, heat oil over medium heat and fry shrimp heads until they turn pink, about 1 minute. Add curry paste and fry until fragrant, about 30 seconds. Add coconut milk and fish sauce. Reduce heat to low and simmer for 10 minutes. Using a slotted spoon, remove and discard shrimp heads. Add shrimp to curry and stir over low heat until shrimp turn pink, 4–5 minutes. Spoon into serving bowls. Garnish each serving with shredded red chili. Serve with steamed jasmine rice.

Serves 4

$1^1/_2$ lb (750 g) jumbo shrimp (king prawns), with heads

1 tablespoon vegetable oil

2 tablespoons Thai red curry paste (see page 14 for recipe)

2 cups (16 fl oz / 500 ml) coconut milk

1 tablespoon fish sauce

1 fresh red Thai or Anaheim chili, seeded and cut into shreds 2-inch (5-cm) long for garnish

Mussel curry

1 tablespoon vegetable oil

1 onion, finely chopped

6 cloves garlic, finely chopped

2 fresh green Thai or Anaheim chilies,
  seeded and chopped

1 teaspoon ground turmeric

$^1/_2$ cup (4 fl oz / 125 ml) white wine vinegar

$1^3/_4$ cups (14 fl oz / 440 ml) coconut milk

2 teaspoons sugar

2 lb (1 kg) mussels, scrubbed and debearded

2 tablespoons chopped fresh cilantro
  (fresh coriander)

sea salt to taste

In a large saucepan, heat oil over medium heat and fry onion, garlic, chilies, and turmeric until fragrant, 2–3 minutes. Add vinegar, coconut milk, sugar, and mussels. Bring to a boil, reduce heat to low, cover, and simmer until mussels have opened, about 6 minutes. Remove from heat and discard any mussels that have not opened. Stir in cilantro and salt. Transfer mussels to serving bowls. Pour sauce over, and serve with steamed rice.

Serves 4

Green fish and oven-roasted potato curry

Preheat oven to 400°F (200°C). Cut each potato into 6 chunks. Put potatoes in an oiled roasting pan and coat with 2 tablespoons of oil. Bake until golden and crisp, about 15 minutes.

Meanwhile, in a wok or large skillet, heat remaining 1 tablespoon of oil over medium heat. Add curry paste and fry for 30 seconds, or until fragrant. Add coconut milk, lime leaves, fish sauce, and fish. Reduce heat to low and simmer for 10–12 minutes, or until fish is opaque throughout. Remove from heat and stir in basil, cilantro, and baked potatoes. Spoon into serving bowls. Serve with steamed jasmine rice.

Serves 4

4 potatoes, peeled

3 tablespoons vegetable oil

2 tablespoons Thai green curry paste
  (see page 14 for recipe)

2 cups (16 fl oz / 500 ml) coconut milk

6 fresh kaffir lime leaves

1 tablespoon fish sauce

1 lb (500 g) swordfish fillets,
  cut into 1¹/₂-inch (4-cm) chunks

2 tablespoons chopped fresh basil leaves

2 tablespoons chopped fresh cilantro
  (fresh coriander)

Indian shrimp curry

1 tablespoon vegetable oil

1 teaspoon chili powder

1 tablespoon ground sweet paprika

1/2 teaspoon ground turmeric

3 cloves garlic, finely chopped

2 teaspoons peeled and grated fresh ginger

1 tablespoon ground coriander

1 teaspoon ground cumin

2 teaspoons packed brown sugar

1 1/4 cups (10 fl oz / 300 ml) water

1 3/4 cups (14 fl oz / 440 ml) coconut milk

1 teaspoon sea salt

2 tablespoons tamarind paste

1 1/2 lb (750 g) jumbo shrimp (king prawns), shelled and deveined, tails intact

In a wok or large skillet, heat oil over medium heat and stir-fry chili powder, paprika, turmeric, garlic, ginger, coriander, and cumin until fragrant, about 30 seconds. Stir in brown sugar and water. Bring to a boil, reduce heat to low and simmer for 5 minutes. Add coconut milk, salt, tamarind paste and shrimp. Stir over medium heat until shrimp turn pink, 4–5 minutes. Remove from heat. Spoon into serving dishes. Serve with steamed basmati rice.

Serves 4

Crispy fried fish

In a food processor, combine onion, garlic, coriander, chili powder, black pepper, lemon juice, salt, and oil. Process to a paste. Place fish fillets in a baking dish and spread onion paste over fish. Cover and refrigerate for 1 hour.

Place flour in a shallow bowl. Coat fish in flour, shaking off excess. In a large wok, heat oil to 375°F (190°C), or until a small bread cube dropped in the oil sizzles and turns golden in 1 minute. Fry the fish in batches until golden, 1–2 minutes. Using a slotted spoon, transfer to paper towels to drain. Serve immediately, with lime and tomato wedges.

Serves 4

1/2 onion, grated

3 cloves garlic, finely chopped

2 teaspoons ground coriander

1/2 teaspoon chili powder

1 teaspoon ground black pepper

1 tablespoon fresh lemon juice

1 teaspoon sea salt

1 tablespoon vegetable oil

4 white fish fillets (6 oz / 185 g each)

1 cup all-purpose (plain) flour

3 cups (24 fl oz / 750 ml) vegetable oil for deep-frying

Sri Lankan seafood curry

FOR SPICE MIXTURE

2 tablespoons vegetable oil

1 teaspoon ground coriander

1 teaspoon ground cumin

1 teaspoon fennel seeds

$1/2$ teaspoon ground cinnamon

1 teaspoon yellow mustard seeds

$1/2$ teaspoon chili pepper flakes

$1/2$ teaspoon ground cloves

1 teaspoon ground cardamom

2 tablespoons vegetable oil

1 lb (500 g) swordfish fillets,
   cut into 2-inch (5-cm) chunks

1 onion, chopped

4 cloves garlic, finely chopped

1 stalk lemongrass (white part only), bruised

2 teaspoons peeled and grated fresh ginger

2 teaspoons ground turmeric

8 fresh curry leaves

14 oz (440 g) can chopped tomatoes

$2/3$ cup (5 fl oz / 160 ml) fish broth

12 jumbo shrimp (king prawns),
   shelled and deveined, tails intact

$5^1/2$ oz (170 g) fresh or lump crabmeat,
   picked over for shell

salt to taste

To make spice mixture: In a skillet, heat oil over medium heat. Add all remaining ingredients and cook, stirring, until fragrant, about 1 minute. Remove from heat and let cool. Put fish in a baking dish. Brush with spice mixture and toss to coat. Cover and refrigerate for 30 minutes.

In a wok or large skillet, heat 1 tablespoon of oil over medium heat and fry onion and garlic until onion is soft, about 1 minute. Stir in lemongrass, ginger, turmeric, and curry leaves and fry for 1 minute. Add tomatoes with their juice, and broth, reduce heat to low, and simmer for 5 minutes.

In a large skillet, heat remaining 1 tablespoon of oil over medium heat and fry fish until lightly browned on each side, 2–3 minutes. Add tomato mixture, shrimp, and crabmeat. Cover and simmer, stirring occasionally, until shrimp are pink, about 5 minutes. Add salt. Spoon into serving bowls. Serve with steamed basmati rice.

Serves 4

Fish and tomato curry

To make spice mixture: In a wok or large skillet, heat oil over medium heat and stir-fry remaining ingredients until fragrant, 1–2 minutes. Add fish, tomatoes with their juice, salt, and sugar. Reduce heat to low, cover, and simmer, stirring occasionally, until fish is opaque throughout, 8–10 minutes. Remove from heat and spoon into serving bowls. Sprinkle with cilantro. Serve with lemon wedges and steamed basmati rice.

Serves 4

FOR SPICE MIXTURE

2 tablespoons vegetable oil

1 onion, finely sliced

3 cloves garlic, finely chopped

1 teaspoon peeled and grated fresh ginger

$\frac{1}{2}$ teaspoon ground turmeric

1 teaspoon ground cumin

2 teaspoons ground coriander

1 teaspoon garam masala
   (see page 15 for recipe)

$\frac{1}{2}$ teaspoon chili powder

1 lb (500 g) white fish fillets,
   cut into 2-inch (5-cm) pieces

13 oz (390 g) canned chopped tomatoes

1 teaspoon sea salt

1 teaspoon sugar

2 tablespoons fresh cilantro
   (fresh coriander) leaves

lemon wedges for serving

l a m b

Coconut beef curry

1 tablespoon vegetable oil

1 tablespoon Asian sesame oil

1 onion, chopped

1 tablespoon peeled and grated fresh ginger

5 cloves garlic, finely chopped

1 tablespoon ground turmeric

1 teaspoon chili powder

1 lb (500 g) lean beef,
  cut into 1-inch (2.5-cm) cubes

1 stalk lemongrass (white part only), bruised

1 cup (8 fl oz / 250 ml) water

1 cup (8 fl oz / 250 ml) coconut milk

6 oz (185 g) green beans,
  trimmed and halved crosswise

2 tablespoons chopped fresh cilantro
  (fresh coriander)

In a wok or large skillet, heat oils over medium heat and fry onion, ginger, and garlic until fragrant, about 1 minute. Add turmeric and chili powder and fry for 30 seconds. Add beef, and cook until beef changes color, 3–4 minutes. Add lemongrass, water, and coconut milk. Bring to a boil, reduce heat to low, and simmer until beef is tender, 10–15 minutes. Add beans and cook for 3 minutes. Remove from heat and stir in cilantro. Spoon into serving bowls. Serve with steamed basmati rice.

Serves 4

Lamb and potato rissoles

To make lamb filling: In a small bowl, stir curry powder, salt, and vinegar together to make a paste. In a wok or large skillet, melt ghee and fry garlic, ginger, and chopped onion until onion is soft, 1–2 minutes. Stir in curry powder, salt, and vinegar. Mix well. Stir in lamb, increase heat to high, and cook until meat changes color, 2–3 minutes. Reduce heat to low, cover, and cook until liquid is absorbed. Remove from heat. Add garam masala, cilantro, mint, and 1/2 chopped onion. Transfer to a bowl and let cool completely.

Cook potatoes in salted boiling water until tender, 8–12 minutes. Drain and mash. Add salt, mint, scallions, and chili. Stir well to blend. Form into 12 patties. Place 1 tablespoonful of meat filling in the center and close potato mixture around filling. Dip in beaten egg, then bread crumbs to coat evenly. Cover and refrigerate for 30 minutes.

In a wok, Dutch oven, or deep fryer, heat oil to 375°F (190°C), or until a small bread cube dropped in the oil sizzles and turns golden in 1 minute. Fry rissoles in batches until golden, 2–3 minutes. Using a slotted spoon, transfer to paper towels to drain. Serve hot.

Makes 12 (serves 4)

FOR LAMB FILLING

2 teaspoons good-quality curry powder

1/2 teaspoon sea salt

1 tablespoon white vinegar

1 tablespoon ghee

2 cloves garlic, finely chopped

1 teaspoon peeled and grated fresh ginger

1 onion, chopped

6 oz (185 g) ground (minced) lamb

1/2 cup (4 fl oz / 125 ml) hot water

1 teaspoon garam masala
   (see page 15 for recipe)

2 tablespoons chopped fresh cilantro
   (fresh coriander)

1 tablespoon chopped fresh mint

extra, 1/2 onion, chopped

2 1/2 lb (1.25 kg) potatoes, peeled and chopped

1 teaspoon sea salt

2 tablespoons chopped fresh mint

3 scallions (shallots / spring onions), chopped

1 fresh green Thai or Anaheim chili,
   seeded and chopped

1 egg, beaten

1 1/2 cups (6 oz / 185 g) dried bread crumbs

3 cups (24 fl oz / 750 ml) vegetable oil for
   deep-frying

Beef rendang

1 onion, coarsely chopped

6 cloves garlic

1 tablespoon peeled and grated fresh ginger

1 teaspoon chili powder

3 teaspoons ground turmeric

3 teaspoons ground coriander

1 tablespoon coconut milk

1 tablespoon vegetable oil

3 whole cloves

1 cinnamon stick

$1^1/_4$ lb (625 g) lean beef,
   cut into 1-inch (2.5-cm) cubes

2 cups (16 fl oz / 500 ml) coconut milk

2 tablespoons tamarind paste

1 teaspoon packed brown sugar

sea salt to taste

To make spice paste: In a food processor, combine all ingredients and process to a smooth paste.

In a wok or large skillet, heat oil over low heat and stir-fry cloves and cinnamon until fragrant, about 1 minute. Add spice paste and cook for 1 minute. Add beef and cook until beef changes color on all sides, 4–5 minutes. Stir in coconut milk and bring to a boil. Reduce heat to low and simmer until beef is tender, 15–20 minutes. Add tamarind, sugar, and salt. Spoon into serving bowls. Serve with steamed basmati rice.

Serves 4

Thai pork and ginger curry

To make spice paste: In a food processor, combine all ingredients and process to a thick paste. Put pork in a medium bowl, add paste, and stir to coat evenly. Cover and refrigerate for 30 minutes. Put ginger in a small bowl, add $\frac{1}{3}$ cup (3 fl oz / 90 ml) of warm water, and let stand for 10 minutes. Drain.

In a wok or large skillet, heat oil over medium heat and sauté pork for 10 minutes. Add remaining 1 cup (8 fl oz / 250 ml) of water, soy sauce, brown sugar, and tamarind paste. Reduce heat to low and simmer for about 15 minutes, or until pork is tender. Add ginger and scallions. Spoon into serving bowls. Garnish with cilantro leaves and serve with steamed jasmine rice.

Serves 4

FOR SPICE PASTE

1 stalk lemongrass (white part only), bruised and chopped

1 tablespoon peeled and grated fresh galangal

3 fresh red Thai or Anaheim chilies, coarsely chopped

1 tablespoon coriander seeds

2 teaspoons dried shrimp paste

6 cloves garlic, coarsely chopped

2 teaspoons ground turmeric

2 teaspoons Asian sesame oil

1 lb (500 g) lean pork, cut into 1-inch (2.5-cm) cubes

$\frac{1}{4}$ cup peeled and finely julienned fresh ginger

$1\frac{1}{3}$ cups (11 fl oz / 340 ml) warm water

2 tablespoons vegetable oil

1 tablespoon soy sauce

1 tablespoon packed brown sugar

2 tablespoons tamarind paste

4 scallions (shallots / spring onions), sliced

2 tablespoons fresh cilantro (fresh coriander)

Spicy lamb

1 tablespoon vegetable oil

4 cardamom pods

1 cinnamon stick

4 whole cloves

1 onion, finely chopped

12 oz (375 g) ground (minced) lamb

2 teaspoons garam masala
  (see page 15 for recipe)

1 teaspoon chili powder

4 cloves garlic, finely chopped

3 teaspoons peeled and grated fresh ginger

1 teaspoon sea salt

6 oz (185 g) potatoes,
  peeled and cut into 1-inch (2.5-cm) cubes

13 oz (390 g) canned chopped tomatoes

1/2 cup (4 fl oz / 125 ml) hot water

2 tablespoons chopped fresh cilantro
  (fresh coriander)

2 tablespoons chopped fresh mint

In a wok or large skillet, heat oil over medium heat and stir-fry cardamom pods, cinnamon stick, and cloves until fragrant, about 1 minute. Add onion and stir-fry until onion is soft, about 2 minutes. Stir in lamb, garam masala, chili powder, garlic, ginger, and salt. Stir-fry until lamb changes color, 4–5 minutes. Add potatoes, tomatoes and their juice, and hot water. Reduce heat to low, cover, and simmer until potatoes are tender, about 8 minutes. Remove from heat and stir in cilantro and mint. Spoon into serving bowls. Serve hot with naan bread or steamed basmati rice.

Serves 4

Green curry pork

In a wok or large skillet, heat oil over medium heat and fry curry paste until fragrant, about 30 seconds. Add pork, and stir-fry until pork changes color, about 2 minutes. Stir in all remaining ingredients. Reduce heat to low and simmer until pork is tender, 12–15 minutes. Spoon into serving bowls. Serve with steamed jasmine rice.

Serves 4

1 tablespoon vegetable oil

3 tablespoons Thai green curry paste (see page 14 for recipe)

1 lb (500 g) lean pork, cut into 1-inch (2-cm) cubes

1 tablespoon green peppercorns

4 fresh green bird's eye or Thai (bird) chilies

2 tablespoons peeled and finely shredded fresh galangal

1 cup (8 fl oz / 250 ml) coconut milk

2 teaspoons fish sauce

2 teaspoons packed brown sugar

4 fresh kaffir lime leaves

Burmese vegetable curry

1 tablespoon vegetable oil

1 tablespoon Asian sesame oil

1 onion, chopped

2 tablespoons peeled and grated fresh ginger

4 cloves garlic, finely chopped

2 teaspoons ground turmeric

2 teaspoons dried shrimp paste

1 lb (500 g) mixed vegetables, such as broccoli, cauliflower, beans, zucchini, and carrots, cut into bite-sized pieces

2 fresh green Thai or Anaheim chilies, seeded and chopped

1¼ cups (10 fl oz / 300 ml) coconut milk

In a wok or large skillet, heat oils over medium heat and fry onion, ginger, and garlic until onion is soft, about 1 minute. Add turmeric and shrimp paste and fry for 1 minute. Add vegetables and chilies and fry for 5 minutes. Add coconut milk, reduce heat to low, and simmer until vegetables are just tender, about 3 minutes. Spoon into serving bowls. Serve with naan bread or steamed jasmine rice.

Serves 2 as a main dish

Curried mashed potato

In a large saucepan of salted boiling water, cook potatoes until tender, 8–12 minutes. Drain and mash. In a small skillet, melt ghee over medium heat and fry mustard seeds until they pop, about 30 seconds. Add chilies and onion and fry until onion is soft, 1–2 minutes. Remove from heat. Stir in turmeric, garam masala, salt, lime juice, and mint. Mix well. Add to mashed potatoes, mixing until well combined. Spoon into a serving dish and drizzle with oil. Serve immediately, with curries.

Serves 4 as a side dish

1½ lb (750 g) potatoes, peeled and chopped

2 tablespoons ghee

1 teaspoon yellow mustard seeds

1 fresh green Thai or Anaheim chili,
   seeded and sliced

1 fresh red Thai or Anaheim chili,
   seeded and sliced

½ onion, chopped

½ teaspoon ground turmeric

1 teaspoon garam masala
   (see page 15 for recipe)

1 teaspoon sea salt

2 tablespoons fresh lime juice

1 tablespoon chopped fresh mint

1 tablespoon olive oil, for drizzling

Spicy cauliflower

3 tablespoons vegetable oil

1 onion, cut into 8 wedges

2 red Thai or Anaheim chilies,
 seeded and chopped

4 cloves garlic, finely chopped

1 teaspoon ground cumin

1 teaspoon dried shrimp paste

1 lb (500 g) cauliflower, cut into florets

1/3 cup (3 fl oz / 90 ml) chicken broth

1 tablespoon sesame seeds, toasted

1 tablespoon fresh cilantro
 (fresh coriander) leaves

In a wok or large skillet, heat oil over medium heat and fry onion, chilies, and garlic until onion is soft, 1–2 minutes. Add cumin and shrimp paste, mashing with the back of a spoon, and fry for 1 minute. Add cauliflower and toss to coat. Add broth, cover, and cook over low heat until cauliflower is tender, 8–10 minutes.

Remove from heat and spoon into a serving dish. Serve immediately, sprinkled with sesame seeds and cilantro leaves.

Serves 2 as an accompaniment

Mango and yogurt curry

In a large, heavy saucepan or wok, heat oil over medium heat and fry mustard seeds, onion, ginger, and chili for 2 minutes, or until onion is soft. Add chili pepper flakes, turmeric, and curry leaves, and cook for 2 minutes. Remove from heat and stir in yogurt. Return to stove and cook over very low heat for 1 minute. Remove from heat, and add mangoes, salt, and mint. Stir until well combined. Serve warm immediately.

Serves 2–4 as a side dish

1 tablespoon vegetable oil

1 teaspoon brown mustard seeds

1 onion, cut into 8 wedges

1 teaspoon peeled and grated fresh ginger

1 large green Thai or Anaheim chili, seeded and sliced

1/4 teaspoon chili pepper flakes

1 teaspoon ground turmeric

12 curry leaves

1 1/2 cups (12 oz / 375 g) plain (natural) yogurt

3 mangoes, peeled, cut from pit, and sliced

sea salt to taste

1 tablespoon chopped fresh mint

Spicy tomato rice

1 cup (7 oz / 220 g) basmati rice

1 tablespoon vegetable oil

1 small onion, chopped

2 cloves garlic, finely chopped

1 fresh red bird's eye or Thai (bird) chili, seeded and chopped

1 teaspoon cumin seeds

6 black peppercorns

2 whole cloves

1 cinnamon stick

$^{1}/_{2}$ cup ($2^{1}/_{2}$ oz / 75 g) fresh or frozen peas

$6^{1}/_{2}$ oz (200 g) canned tomatoes

2 tablespoons tomato paste (puree)

$1^{3}/_{4}$ cups (14 fl oz / 440 ml) boiling water

2 tablespoons chopped fresh cilantro (fresh coriander)

sea salt to taste

Rinse rice in several changes of cold water until water runs clear. Put into a bowl, cover with cold water, and let stand for 5 minutes. Drain and set aside.

In a wok or large, heavy saucepan, heat oil over medium heat and fry onion, garlic, and chili until onion is soft, 1–2 minutes. Add cumin seeds, peppercorns, cloves, and cinnamon stick and cook for 2 minutes. Stir in rice, peas, tomatoes, and tomato paste, and cook for 2 minutes, stirring until well combined. Add boiling water, cover, and reduce heat to low. Simmer until rice is tender and all liquid has been absorbed, 10–12 minutes. Remove from heat and let stand for 10 minutes. With a fork, stir in cilantro and salt. Remove whole cloves and cinnamon stick. Spoon into serving bowls and serve immediately.

Serves 4 as an accompaniment

Indian pilaf

Rinse rice in several changes of cold water until water runs clear. Put rice in a bowl and add cold water to cover. Let stand for 30 minutes. Drain.

In a medium, heavy saucepan, heat oil over medium heat and fry onion and garlic until onion is soft, 1–2 minutes. Stir in fennel, sesame seeds, turmeric, cumin, salt, cloves, cardamom pods, and peppercorns. Fry until fragrant, 1–2 minutes. Add drained rice, and fry, stirring constantly, for 2 minutes, or until rice is opaque. Pour in broth and bring to a boil. Cover, reduce heat to low, and simmer until rice is tender and all liquid has been absorbed, 15–20 minutes. Remove from heat and let stand, covered, for 5 minutes. Spoon into serving bowls and garnish with curry leaves.

Serves 4 as an accompaniment

$1^1/_4$ cups (9 oz / 280 g) basmati rice
1 tablespoon vegetable oil
1 onion, chopped
2 cloves garlic, finely chopped
1 teaspoon fennel seeds
1 tablespoon sesame seeds
$^1/_2$ teaspoon ground turmeric
1 teaspoon ground cumin
$^1/_2$ teaspoon sea salt
2 whole cloves
3 cardamom pods, lightly crushed
6 black peppercorns
$1^3/_4$ cups (14 fl oz / 440 ml) chicken broth
fresh curry leaves for garnish

Garlic and cumin seed rice

3 tablespoons vegetable oil

4 cloves garlic, finely chopped

3 bay leaves

2 teaspoons cumin seeds

1¹/₂ cups (10¹/₂ oz / 330 g) basmati rice

2¹/₂ cups (20 fl oz / 625 ml) water

In a wok or large, heavy saucepan, heat oil over medium heat and fry garlic until fragrant but not browned, about 1 minute. Add bay leaves and cumin seeds and cook for 1 minute. Add rice and stir-fry until rice is opaque, about 2 minutes. Add water, stir, cover and bring to a boil. Reduce heat to low, and cook, stirring occasionally, until rice is tender, 10–15 minutes. Let stand, covered, for 5 minutes. Remove bay leaves. Serve as an accompaniment to curries.

Serves 4

Bhaturas (deep-fried puris)

Sift flour and salt into a medium bowl. Stir in oil, yogurt, and enough water to make a soft dough. Cover with a tea towel and let stand for 15 minutes. Turn out dough onto a floured board, and knead until smooth, about 3–4 minutes. Divide into 10 pieces and form each into a ball. Using a rolling pin, roll each ball of dough into a 6-inch (15-cm) round.

In a wok or deep fryer, heat oil to 375°F (190°C), or until a small bread cube dropped in the oil sizzles and turns golden in 1 minute. Add dough rounds in batches and fry until puffed and golden, about 1 minute; then turn and cook for 30 seconds. Using a slotted spoon, transfer to paper towels to drain. Serve hot or at room temperature, with curries.

Makes 10

1 1/4 cups (6 1/2 oz / 220 g) self-rising flour
1 teaspoon sea salt
1 tablespoon vegetable oil
1 tablespoon plain (natural) yogurt
3–4 tablespoons (2 fl oz / 60 ml) water
3 cups (24 fl oz / 750 ml) vegetable oil
   for deep-frying

Chapatis

2 cups (10 oz / 300 g) atta flour or
  whole-wheat (wholemeal) flour

$\frac{1}{2}$ teaspoon sea salt

about $\frac{3}{4}$ cup (6 fl oz / 180 ml) water

1 tablespoon vegetable oil

Sift flour and salt into a large bowl. Stir in enough water to make a firm dough. Turn out onto a floured board and knead until smooth, about 5 minutes. Put dough in a medium bowl, cover with a damp tea towel, and let stand for 1 hour. Knead again for 2–3 minutes. Divide dough into 12 portions and form each into a ball. Roll out each ball into a 6-inch (15-cm) round.

Heat a nonstick skillet over medium heat and brush lightly with oil. Cook 1 chapati until it bubbles, turn over and cook until golden, pressing down with a large spoon. Repeat with remaining chapati. Serve warm, with curries.

Hint

Chapatis are best made just before eating, but they can also be wrapped in aluminum foil and reheated in a warm oven.

Naan

In a small bowl, combine yeast, 1 teaspoon of sugar, ¼ cup (2 fl oz / 60 ml) warm water, and ½ cup (2½ oz / 75 g) of flour. Cover and let stand until foamy, about 10 minutes. Sift remaining 3 cups (15 oz / 470 g) of flour and 2 teaspoons of sugar into a large bowl. Make a well in the center and pour in yeast mixture, yogurt, remaining ¼ cup warm water, cumin, egg, ghee, and salt. Stir until combined. Turn out onto a floured board and knead until smooth and elastic, about 7 minutes. Put dough in a lightly oiled bowl and turn to coat. Cover with a damp tea towel and let rise in a warm place until doubled in bulk, about 45 minutes.

Preheat oven to 400°F (200°C). Line 2 baking sheets with parchment (baking) paper.

Punch down dough, turn out onto a floured board, and knead until smooth, 6–8 minutes. Divide into 8 pieces and form into balls. Cover and let rest for 5 minutes. Roll each ball into a 6-inch (15-cm) round. Spread each round with 1 tablespoon of yogurt, and sprinkle with cumin seeds. Place on prepared baking sheets and bake until golden and crisp, 12–15 minutes. Serve warm.

Makes 8

1 oz (30 g) compressed fresh yeast, crumbled

3 teaspoons sugar

½ cup (4 fl oz / 125 ml) warm water

3½ cups (17½ oz / 535 g) all-purpose (plain) flour

¼ cup (2 oz / 60 g) plain (natural) yogurt, plus extra ½ cup (4 oz / 125 g)

½ teaspoon ground cumin

1 egg, beaten

2 oz (60 g) ghee, melted

2 teaspoons sea salt

2 tablespoons black cumin seeds

Hint

This naan bread recipe is a traditional Indian favorite. Serve warm with Chicken vindaloo (see recipe page 25).

Carrot and honey sambal

¹/₃ cup (3 fl oz / 90 ml) fresh lemon juice

1 tablespoon honey

12 oz (375 g) carrots, peeled and shredded

2 tablespoons vegetable oil

¹/₂ teaspoon chili pepper flakes

3 fresh curry leaves

sea salt to taste

In a medium bowl, combine lemon juice and honey and stir until honey is dissolved. Add shredded carrot, and toss to coat well. Heat oil in a small, heavy saucepan over medium heat and fry chili pepper flakes and curry leaves until fragrant, about 30 seconds. Pour over carrot mixture. Add salt and mix well. Refrigerate for 1–2 hours to chill. Serve as a side dish, with curries.

Serves 2–4

Tomato and mint salad

In a medium bowl, combine tomatoes, scallions, and mint. In a screwtop jar, combine lemon juice, sugar, chili powder, and salt. Shake until well combined. Pour over tomato mixture and stir gently to coat. Refrigerate for 15 minutes before serving. Serve as a side dish, with curries.

Serves 4

4 tomatoes, cut into thin wedges

6 scallions (shallots/spring onions), including some green parts, sliced

2 tablespoons chopped fresh mint

1/4 cup (2 fl oz/60 ml) fresh lemon juice

2 teaspoons sugar

1/4 teaspoon chili powder

1/2 teaspoon sea salt

Coconut sambal

In a food processor, combine coconut, milk, chilies, sugar, ginger, and yogurt. Process for about 20 seconds, or until blended. Transfer to a serving dish and add salt.

In a wok or small skillet, heat oil over medium heat and fry mustard seeds and curry leaves until mustard seeds begin to pop. Remove from heat and pour over coconut mixture. Refrigerate for 1–2 hours to chill. Serve as a side dish, with curries.

Serves 2–4

1 cup unsweetened, shredded dried (dessicated) coconut

2 tablespoons hot milk

2 fresh green Thai or Anaheim chilies, seeded and coarsely chopped

1 teaspoon sugar

2 teaspoons peeled and grated fresh ginger

1/2 cup (4 oz/125 g) plain (natural) yogurt

sea salt to taste

2 tablespoons vegetable oil

2 teaspoons brown mustard seeds

6 fresh curry leaves

Bananas in yogurt

¹/₄ cup (1 oz / 30 g) unsweetened, shredded dried
  (dessicated) coconut

1 tablespoon hot water

1 cup (8 oz / 250 g) plain (natural) yogurt

2 tablespoons fresh lemon juice

2 teaspoons sugar

¹/₂ teaspoon sea salt

3 bananas, peeled and cut crosswise into slices

1 teaspoon ghee

1 teaspoon cumin seeds

1 teaspoon brown mustard seeds

In a medium bowl, combine coconut and water, and mix well. Add yogurt, lemon juice, sugar, and salt. Mix until well combined. Stir in bananas. In a small skillet, melt ghee over medium heat and fry cumin and mustard seeds until mustard seeds pop. Remove from heat and stir into banana mixture. Chill, and serve as a side dish with curries.

Serves 2–4

Cucumber and yogurt sambal

2 tablespoons unsweetened, shredded dried
  (dessicated) coconut

2 tablespoons hot water

¹/₂ English (hothouse) cucumber,
  peeled and seeded

1 fresh green Thai or Anaheim chili,
  seeded and chopped

¹/₂ teaspoon sea salt

³/₄ cup (6 oz / 180 g) plain (natural) yogurt

1 teaspoon ghee

¹/₂ teaspoon brown mustard seeds

3 fresh curry leaves

In a medium bowl, combine coconut and hot water, and mix well. Shred cucumber, and add to the bowl with chili, salt, and yogurt. Mix well. In a small, heavy saucepan, melt ghee over medium heat and fry mustard seeds and curry leaves until mustard seeds pop, about 30 seconds. Remove from heat and stir into cucumber mixture. Refrigerate for 1–2 hours to chill. Serve as a side dish, with curries.

Serves 2–4

Fruit lassis (yogurt drinks)

In a blender or food processor, combine yogurt, milk, and 1 cup (8 oz / 250 g) of the chopped fruit. Process until frothy, about 20 seconds. Add sugar. Fill glasses with crushed ice, pour in yogurt mixture, and top each with a portion of the remaining ½ cup (4 oz / 125 g) of chopped fruit. Garnish with fruit, flowers, or leaves.

Serves 4

1 cup (8 oz / 250 g) plain (natural) yogurt
1 cup (8 fl oz / 250 ml) milk
1½ cups (12 oz / 375 g) chopped fresh fruit
　(peach, mango, or raspberry)
sugar to taste
crushed ice cubes
fresh fruit, leaves, or flowers for garnish

Hint

A lassi is a refreshing drink to enjoy with hot and spicy meals.

glossary

Almonds: The nut of the almond tree. Available without shells, blanched, whole, flaked or slithered.

Atta flour: A fine wholemeal flour made from low gluten, soft-textured wheat. Also known as chapati flour. Sold in Indian stores.

Besan flour: A pale yellow flour made from chick peas. Available from Indian stores.

Bruise: To crush food partially, particularly a herb, to release its flavor. Bruised food or herbs can be removed before serving.

Chicken stock: Use homemade or commercially made liquid stock. Available at supermarkets.

Chinese powdered red food coloring: A deep red powder, traditionally used to color Chinese barbecued pork. Sold as a food coloring and is available from Asian supermarkets. Use in small quantities. Add to marinades to color food prior to cooking.

Coconut milk and cream: When grated coconut flesh is steeped in water, it yields a rich liquid called coconut milk. The thick substances that rise to the top of coconut milk form coconut cream. Coconut milk and cream are available in cans in the supermarket

Coriander, ground: The tiny yellow-tan seeds of the cilantro (coriander) plant. Used whole or ground as a spice.

Cumin, ground: Also known as comino. The small crescent-shaped seeds have an earthy, nutty flavor. Available whole or ground.

Fenugreek, ground: The seed of an aromatic plant of the pea family, native to the Mediterranean region. Has a bittersweet, burnt sugar after taste, available whole or ground.

Fish sauce: Pungent sauce of salted, fermented fish and other seasonings, used in cooking and as a dipping sauce. Also known as nam pla.

Garam masala: A blend of spices, cardamom, cumin, coriander, cinnamon, cloves and pepper. Store away from sunlight. Use Garam masala (see page 15 for recipe) for an original homemade curry flavor if you have the time.

Ghee: A form of clarified fat or pure butter fat, originating in India. Has a high smoke point and nutty, caramel-like flavor.

Grinding: A milling process, during which the spices or food products are reduced to a powder, by using a mortar and pestle, coffee/spice grinder or food processor.

Lassi: Hindi for a cold beverage made from yogurt thinned with water or milk, sweetened and flavored with rose water or fruit.

Paprika: A blend of dried red skinned chilies. The flavor can range from slightly sweet and mild to pungent and hot.

Peanut: A legume, not a nut. It is a plant's nut-like seed that grows underground. Available raw, roasted, salted or unsalted.

Pilaf: A cooking method for grains. The grains are lightly sautéed in oil, then hot liquid is added, the mixture is then simmered until all liquid is absorbed.

Puree: To process food to achieve a smooth pulp.

Sambal: A fresh or cooked relish served in small quantities to add zest to a meal.

Shrimp paste: A pungent paste made from fermented shrimps (prawns). It has a pungent odor, but its flavor is unique to Asian cooking. Shrimp paste is always heated, fried, or grilled before adding to a dish. Also known as blanchan, blacan or kapi.

Soy sauce: A sauce made from fermented boiled soybeans and roasted wheat or barley. There are many different varieties of soy, but they mainly fit into two categories, light or dark. Light is thinner and saltier and used more for dipping. Dark soy is thicker, darker and less salty than light soy, and is used more in cooking.

Spring roll wrappers: Traditionally used in Asian cooking to encase meat, vegetable or noodle fillings. Spring roll wrappers are rolled into a cigar shape and deep-fried until golden and crisp. Sometimes called spring roll skins. These thin, lacy wrappers are sold frozen in the supermarket. They should be defrosted and separated before using. It's best to keep wrappers under a damp cloth while preparing.

Star anise: The dried eight-pointed star-shaped seed pod of a tree belonging to the magnolia family. Star anise is one of the ingredients of Chinese five spice powder. It is also used whole, in segments or ground in Asian cooking. It has an intense liquorice flavor.

Tamarind puree: The puree of a fruit from a tree native to Asia and northern Africa. The long pods contain seeds and a sweet-sour pulp that is dried and sold in blocks or in jars as a puree. If tamarind is only available in block form, simply soak a small section in hot water for 3 minutes to soften, squeezing and kneading the pulp to disperse it in the water. Then strain and measure before use.

Thai sweet chili sauce: Mild chili sauce with a sweet after taste, available in supermarket. Used in cooking and as a dipping sauce to many Asian foods.

Turmeric: A dried, powdery spice produced from the rhizome of a tropical plant related to ginger. It has a strong, spicy flavor and yellow color. Also known as Indian saffron.

Vindaloo: A spicy Indian dish consisting of meat or chicken usually served over rice.

index

Almonds 58

Atta flour 58

Bananas in yogurt 56

Bay leaves 10

Beef

coconut curry 38

rendang 40

Besan flour 58

Bhaturas 51

Bird's-eye chilies 12

Black cumin seeds 9

Bread

bhaturas (deep-fried puris) 51

chapatis 52

naan 53

Bruising 58

Burmese vegetable curry 44

Cardamom 9

Carrot and honey sambal 54

Cauliflower, spicy 46

Chapatis 52

Chicken

chili curry 23

and nut curry 29

and pumpkin curry, Thai 28

tandoori 26

vindaloo 25

Chicken stock 58

Chili-chicken curry 23

Chili pepper flakes 12

Chili powder 12

Chili sauce 58

Chilies 12, 13

Chinese powdered red food

colouring 58

Cilantro 10

Cinnamon sticks 9

Cloves 9

Coconut beef curry 38

Coconut milk and cream 58

Coconut sambal 55

Coriander (cilantro) 10

Coriander seeds 9, 58

Crisps, rice flour 22

Crispy fried fish 35

Cucumber and yogurt sambal 56

Cumin seeds 9, 58

and garlic rice 50

Curried mashed potato 45

Curried mixed nuts 17

Curries

beef rendang 40

Burmese vegetable 44

chicken and nut 29

chicken vindaloo 25

chili-chicken 23

coconut beef 38

duck and green chili 24

festive duck 30

fish and tomato 37

green fish and oven-roasted

potato 33

green pork 43

Indian shrimp 34

mango and yogurt 47

mussel 32

Penang duck 27

spicy cauliflower 46

spicy lamb 42

Sri Lankan seafood 36

Thai chicken and pumpkin 28

Thai pork and ginger 41

Thai red shrimp 31

Curry leaves 10

Curry pastes 12-15

Thai green, Thai red 14

Curry vegetable spring rolls 21

Curry yogurt soup 20

Dal, spicy 16

Deep-fried puris 51

Dried chilies 13

Drinks, yogurt (fruit lassis) 57

Duck

festive curry 30

and green chili curry 24

Penang curry 27

Equipment 11

Fenugreek 58

Festive duck curry 30

Fish

cakes, Thai curry 19

crispy fried 35

green curry 33

and oven-roasted potato

green curry 33

and tomato curry 37

Fish sauce 58

Flour, types of 58

Food colouring 58

Food processor 11

Fruit lassis 57

Galangal 10

Garam masala 15, 58

Garlic and cumin seed rice 50

Ghee 58

Ginger 10

Green curry

fish and oven-roasted

potato 33

paste 14

pork 43

Green peppercorns 9

Grinding 58

Honey and carrot sambal 54

Indian pilaf 49
Indian shrimp curry 34
Ingredients 9-10

Kaffir lime leaves 10

Lamb
    and potato rissoles 39
    spicy 42
Lassis 58
    fruit 57
Lemongrass 10
Lentils, spicy dal 16

Mango and yogurt curry 47
Mashed potato, curried 45
Mint 10
Mortar and pestle 11
Mussel curry 32
Mustard seeds 9

Naan 53
Nuts
    and chicken curry 29
    curried mixed 17

Paprika 58
Peanuts 58
Penang curry
    duck 27
    paste 15
Peppercorns, green 9
Pilaf 58
    Indian 49
Pork
    and ginger Thai curry 41

green curry 43
Potato
    curried mashed 45
    and lamb rissoles 39
    oven-roasted, and fish green
        curry 33
Prawns *see* Shrimp
Pumpkin and chicken curry, Thai 28
Puree, definition 58
Puris, deep-fried 51

Red curry
    paste 14
    Thai shrimp 31
Red food colouring 58
Red lentils, spicy dal 16
Rendang, beef 40
Rice
    garlic and cumin seed 50
    Indian pilaf 49
    spicy tomato 48
Rice flour crisps 22
Rissoles, lamb and potato 39

Salad, tomato and mint 55
Sambal 58
    carrot and honey 54
    coconut 55
    cucumber and yogurt 56
Seafood curry, Sri Lankan 36
Shrimp
    fries 18
    Indian curry 34
    Thai red curry 31
Shrimp paste 58
Soup, curry yogurt 20
Soy sauce 58
Spice grinder 11
Spicy cauliflower 46
Spicy dal 16
Spicy lamb 42
Spicy tomato rice 48

Spring rolls
    curry vegetable 21
    wrappers 58
Sri Lankan seafood curry 36
Star anise 58
Sweet chili sauce 58

Tamarind puree 58
Tandoori chicken 26
Thai chicken and pumpkin curry 28
Thai chilies 13
Thai curry fish cakes 19
Thai green curry paste 14
Thai pork and ginger curry 41
Thai red curry paste 14
Thai red curry shrimp 31
Thai sweet chili sauce 58
Tomato
    and fish curry 37
    and mint salad 55
    spicy rice 48
Turmeric 58

Vegetables
    Burmese curry 44
    curry spring rolls 21
Vindaloo 58
    chicken 25

Wok 11

Yogurt
    bananas in 56
    and cucumber sambal 56
    curry soup 20
    drinks 57
    and mango curry 47

Guide to weights and measures

The conversions given in the recipes in this book are approximate. Whichever system you use, remember to follow it consistently, thereby ensuring that the proportions are consistent throughout a recipe.

WEIGHTS

Imperial	Metric
$\frac{1}{3}$ oz	10 g
$\frac{1}{2}$ oz	15 g
$\frac{3}{4}$ oz	20 g
1 oz	30 g
2 oz	60 g
3 oz	90 g
4 oz ($\frac{1}{4}$ lb)	125 g
5 oz ($\frac{1}{3}$ lb)	150 g
6 oz	180 g
7 oz	220 g
8 oz ($\frac{1}{2}$ lb)	250 g
9 oz	280 g
10 oz	300 g
11 oz	330 g
12 oz ($\frac{3}{4}$ lb)	375 g
16 oz (1 lb)	500 g
2 lb	1 kg
3 lb	1.5 kg
4 lb	2 kg

VOLUME

Imperial	Metric	Cup
1 fl oz	30 ml	
2 fl oz	60 ml	$\frac{1}{4}$
3 fl oz	90 ml	$\frac{1}{3}$
4 fl oz	125 ml	$\frac{1}{2}$
5 fl oz	150 ml	$\frac{2}{3}$
6 fl oz	180 ml	$\frac{3}{4}$
8 fl oz	250 ml	1
10 fl oz	300 ml	$1\frac{1}{4}$
12 fl oz	375 ml	$1\frac{1}{2}$
13 fl oz	400 ml	$1\frac{2}{3}$
14 fl oz	440 ml	$1\frac{3}{4}$
16 fl oz	500 ml	2
24 fl oz	750 ml	3
32 fl oz	1L	4

USEFUL CONVERSIONS

$\frac{1}{4}$ teaspoon	1.25 ml
$\frac{1}{2}$ teaspoon	2.5 ml
1 teaspoon	5 ml
1 Australian tablespoon	20 ml (4 teaspoons)
1 UK/US tablespoon	15 ml (3 teaspoons)

Butter/Shortening

1 tablespoon	$\frac{1}{2}$ oz	15 g
$1\frac{1}{2}$ tablespoons	$\frac{3}{4}$ oz	20 g
2 tablespoons	1 oz	30 g
3 tablespoons	$1\frac{1}{2}$ oz	45 g

OVEN TEMPERATURE GUIDE

The Celsius (°C) and Fahrenheit (°F) temperatures in this chart apply to most electric ovens. Decrease by 25°F or 10°C for a gas oven or refer to the manufacturer's temperature guide. For temperatures below 325°F (160°C), do not decrease the given temperature.

Oven description	°C	°F	Gas Mark
Cool	110	225	$\frac{1}{4}$
	130	250	$\frac{1}{2}$
Very slow	140	275	1
	150	300	2
Slow	170	325	3
Moderate	180	350	4
	190	375	5
Moderately Hot	200	400	6
Fairly Hot	220	425	7
Hot	230	450	8
Very Hot	240	475	9
Extremely Hot	250	500	10

First published in the United States in 2002 by Periplus Editions (HK) Ltd., with editorial offices at 153 Milk Street, Boston, Massachusetts 02109 and 130 Joo Seng Road #06-01/03 Olivine Building Singapore 368357

Commissioned by Deborah Nixon; Text: Vicki Liley; Photographer: Ben Dearnley; Stylist: Vicki Liley; Design Concepts: Kerry Klinner; Editor: Carolyn Miller; Production Manager: Sally Stokes; Project Co-ordinator: Alexandra Nahlous

Printed in India